Table of Contents

I0474111

FILING FOR
BANKRUPTCY IN CALIFORNIA
MADE SIMPLE

A Guide to Help You Decide- 2012 Edition

by
Theodore W. Connolly

DISCLAIMER

This publication is designed to provide general information regarding the subject matter covered. However, rules, regulations, laws, practices and the interpretation of same often change or vary from state to state and court to court, particularly with regard to bankruptcy laws. Because each situation is different, the reader is advised to consult with a lawyer regarding that individual's specific situation. Neither the author nor the publisher assume any responsibility for any errors or omissions, nor do they represent or warrant that the information, ideas, plans, actions, suggestions, and methods of operation contained herein is in all cases true, accurate, appropriate, or legal. It is the reader's responsibility to consult with his or her own lawyer before putting any of the enclosed information, ideas, or practices into play. The authors and the publisher specifically disclaim any liability resulting from the use or application of the information contained in this book, and the information is not intended to serve as legal advice related to individual situations.

This book is a work of the author's experience and opinion. Names, characters, places and incidents are either the product of the author's imagination or are used fictitiously. Any resemblance to actual persons, living or dead, or to actual events or locales is entirely coincidental.

FILING FOR BANKRUPTCY IN CALIFORNIA MADE SIMPLE

Visit the author's website:
http://www.theodoreconnolly.com;
http://www.roadoutofdebt.com and
www.filingmadesimple.com.

Introduction

By choosing to read this easy and essential guide on filing bankruptcy in California, you have taken a great step out of debt and towards understanding bankruptcy. Don't be fooled by the size of the guide. You will not find the filler you would normally find in other books. Instead, you will get the facts about filing for bankruptcy along with tips and insight you will not find anywhere else.

Far too often, people file for bankruptcy unaware of what may happen and how bankruptcy will actually affect their debts and assets. After reading this simple guide, you will be able to make a well-informed decision about filing for bankruptcy.

You will learn the basics of bankruptcy and what will happen to your property in your bankruptcy case. Bankruptcy provides great benefits, but it has downsides as well. The only way to know whether bankruptcy is right for you is to understand what bankruptcy can and cannot do for you in your unique circumstances.

By reading this guide, you will save yourself hours and hours of stress and agony wondering about whether bankruptcy can help you. And, what you learn could save you hundreds, or more likely, thousands of dollars.

The thought of filing a personal bankruptcy case may make you cringe, but it shouldn't. You should look at it as you would any major financial decision, such as buying a house, buying a car, or taking a vacation. You should consider how filing for bankruptcy may affect your life, how *not* filing may affect your life, and then decide which results are better for you. The only way to do this in California is to know the true consequences before you file.

This Guide Makes it Simple to Decide

This Guide is filled with plain language, simple explanations, flow charts, and checklists so that you will understand what will happen and what to do as simply and easily as possible.

I wrote this guide because I want you to succeed. I want you to find a way out of debt.

Who am I? I am a bankruptcy and finance lawyer with years of experience helping people deal with debt and financial problems who has overcome my own personal finance challenges. I am co-author of the book, *The Road Out of Debt: Bankruptcy and Other Solutions to Your Financial Problems,* which I wrote with Joan Feeney, a bankruptcy judge on the United States Bankruptcy Court for the District of Massachusetts.

My collaboration with Judge Feeney on our first book allowed me to learn from her decades of knowledge and command of bankruptcy. Her advice and teaching built the foundation, so that I could put together this simple and authoritative guide.

I recommend consulting my first book, the *Road Out of Debt, for more in-depth information* beyond what this Guide gives you. The *Road Out of Debt* is a total package that walks you through all the steps to get out of debt, with or without filing for bankruptcy, and helps you understand whether filing for bankruptcy is right for you. It costs a little more, but it is worth it for the savings it will bring you in your life.

If you are considering bankruptcy and need some quick answers about bankruptcy, this no-nonsense guide will take away the mysteries of filing for bankruptcy in California in a short, simple package. Whether you decide that filing bankruptcy is your best route or not, you have taken a giant step towards getting out of debt and removing unnecessary stress from your life. I wish you the best of luck in your fight!

Chapter 1

QUICK ANSWERS TO YOUR BANKRUPTCY QUESTIONS

A. Am I Eligible to File for Bankruptcy?

If you live in or have property in the United States, you can file a "bankruptcy petition." A bankruptcy petition is a collection of official forms and documents that start your bankruptcy case. The forms and documents that you need to file are set out in the Checklist in Chapter 3.

B. Where Can I File for Bankruptcy?

Bankruptcy cases cannot be commenced in state courts. Instead, you file a bankruptcy petition with the clerk of the bankruptcy court.

You can file in California if you lived in California for the 730 days before you file your bankruptcy petition, or if California was the state of your residence for the majority of the 180 days prior to the 730 days before filing your bankruptcy petition. Otherwise, you have to file in the state in which you lived for the majority of the 180-day period that precedes the 730 days before you file for bankruptcy.

California has the following bankruptcy courts:

**California Central Bankruptcy Court
(Main Office)**

Edward R. Roybal Federal Building and Courthouse
255 East Temple Street
Los Angeles CA 90012-3332
Phone
213-894-3118

California Central Bankruptcy Court

3420 Twelfth Street
Riverside CA 92501-3801
Phone
951-774-1000

California Central Bankruptcy Court

Ronald Reagan Federal Building and
United States Courthouse
411 West Fourth Street
Santa Ana CA 92701
Phone
714-338-5300
California Central Bankruptcy Court

Federal Building
1415 State Street
Santa Barbara CA 93101-2511
Phone
805-884-4800
California Central Bankruptcy Court

Warner Center
21041 Burbank Boulevard
Woodland Hills CA 91367-6609
Phone
818-587-2900

California Eastern Bankruptcy Court

Robert E. Coyle United States Courthouse
2500 Tulare Street, Suite 2501
Fresno CA 93721

Phone
559-499-5800

California Eastern Bankruptcy Court

1200 I Street, Suite C
Modesto CA 95354-0836
Phone
209-521-5160

**California Eastern Bankruptcy Court
(Main Office)**

Robert T. Matsui United States Courthouse
501 I Street, Room 3-200
Sacramento CA 95814-7300
Phone
916-930-4400

California Northern Bankruptcy Court

United States Courthouse
1300 Clay Street, 3rd Floor
Oakland CA 94612-1425
Mailing Address
PO Box 2070
Oakland CA 94612-1425
Phone
510-879-3600

**California Northern Bankruptcy Court
(Main Office)**

United States Courthouse
235 Pine Street, 19th Floor
San Francisco CA 94104-2716

Mailing Address
PO Box 7341
San Francisco CA 94104-2716
Phone
415-268-2300

California Northern Bankruptcy Court

Robert F. Peckham Federal Building and
United States Courthouse
280 South First Street, Room 3035
San Jose CA 95113-3002
Phone
408-278-7500

California Northern Bankruptcy Court

United States Courthouse
99 South E Street
Santa Rosa CA 95404-6517
Phone
707-547-5900

**California Southern Bankruptcy Court
(Main Office)**

Jacob Weinberger United States Courthouse
325 West F Street
San Diego CA 92101-6017
Phone
619-557-5620

The bankruptcy court where you file your documents is
most likely the one closest to your home. However, if you
have any doubts, call the court to confirm. Also, many
states have hearings and meetings in locations in addition

to the bankruptcy court locations, so read any notices from the court very carefully.

C. What are the Different Types of Bankruptcy?

The different types of bankruptcy are called chapters. Three different Chapters of bankruptcy are available to an individual: Chapter 7, Chapter 13, and Chapter 11.

Most People File Chapter 7 Bankruptcy Cases

Each bankruptcy Chapter has requirements or restrictions. I discuss the different Chapters in detail later in the book.

D. What do I need to know about a Chapter 7 bankruptcy case?

Here are some typical questions about Chapter 7 bankruptcy cases.

Q: What are the important prerequisites of Chapter 7?

A: You need to pass a means test to qualify. See Chapter 2 for more information on means tests.

Q: Usual length?

A: 3–6 months.

Q. When is Chapter 7 my best bet?

A: Chapter 7 is typically your best bet when your debts are beginning to overwhelm you, you don't own a house (or you own a house and are current on your payments) and your monthly expenses and debts will exceed you monthly income for the foreseeable future. If you want to keep your home and are not current on mortgage payments, you will have to consider a Chapter 13 bankruptcy case.

Q: How do I succeed in a Chapter 7 bankruptcy case?

A: You succeed in a Chapter 7 bankruptcy case when you are completely honest in your filings with the bankruptcy court and you are determined to make necessary financial changes in your life.

Q: How does Chapter 7 work?

A: In principle, all your non-exempt assets are evaluated and marshaled by a trustee and sold to pay your creditors as much of your debt as possible. In practice, most debtors do not lose any assets and do not have any assets sold to satisfy creditors.

E. What do I need to know about a Chapter 13 bankruptcy case?

Here are some typical questions about Chapter 13 bankruptcy cases.

Q: What are the important prerequisites of Chapter 13?

A: You must have a wage or steady stream of income.

Q: Usual length?

A: 3 months of the actual case, and then you enter into a 3- to 5-year payment plan.

Q: When is Chapter 13 my best bet?

A: Chapter 13 is typically your best bet if your debts are getting the best of you, you are trying to hold onto a house and your other assets and you have money left over each month after paying your essential monthly expenses.

Q: How do I succeed in a Chapter 13 bankruptcy case?

A: For success in a Chapter 13, you should have some money left over each month after necessary expenses to pay your creditors at a reduced rate over a 3- to 5-year plan.

Q: How does Chapter 13 work?

A: At the beginning of your case, you set up a court-approved payment plan over three to five years that provides your creditors equal or more payment than they would have received if you had filed Chapter 7.

F. What Does it Cost to File for Bankruptcy?

The filing and administrative fees for bankruptcy cases are:

$306 for Chapter 7 cases;

$281 for Chapter 13; and

$1,046 for Chapter 11 cases.

These fees are in addition to attorney fees and credit counseling fees. You may file an application to pay the filing fees in installments or ask the bankruptcy court for a waiver of the filing fees.

G. How Do I File for Bankruptcy?

If you file your petition on your own, you will have to file in person at the clerk's office at the bankruptcy court that covers where you live or where you own property.

If you a hire a lawyer or a filing service, the lawyer or filing service will file your petition online through the bankruptcy court's website/electronic filing service.

H. What Happens to My Debts?

It depends on the type of debt and on your bankruptcy case. Also, some debts are "non-dischargeable," which means that your bankruptcy case will not affect them. The different treatments of the different debts are discussed throughout the Guide.

I. What Will Happen If I Own a Home?

Whether you can keep your home, make up for any defaults and other possibilities depends upon several factors and the bankruptcy Chapter under which you file. See Chapter 12.

J. What Will Happen if I Own a Motor Vehicle or Boat?

What happens to your car or boat depends upon several factors and the bankruptcy Chapter under which you file. See Chapter 13.

K. Is There Anything I Need to do Before Filing for Bankruptcy?

Yes. One prerequisite is taking a credit counseling session. You can take it in person, online or sometimes over the phone, but you must take it within 180 days of filing (very limited exceptions apply). You should also learn about bankruptcy options from information in the *Road Out of Debt* and other resources; talking to a bankruptcy attorney or an honest credit counselor can also be very helpful. See the Checklist in Chapter 3 for more information. Plus, if you own a house, make sure you have declared a homestead in compliance with the laws of California.

L. Will I Have to go to Court?

Not likely, but you will have to appear in front of a trustee to discuss your bankruptcy case under oath. This is called a "341 meeting" or creditor's meeting. See the Checklist in Chapter 3 for more information.

M. Why Would I Have to Appear in Front of a Judge in Court?

There are many reasons. If you have a lawyer, your lawyer will most likely appear on your behalf. Some of the reasons you (or your lawyer) would appear in court include:

Eliminating a lien on your property.

Fighting against a creditor who wants to take action against your secured property or objects to its debt being included in your bankruptcy case discharge.

The U.S. trustee doesn't believe you were honest filling out your bankruptcy petition or other filing.

You want to reaffirm a debt on your car (you will likely have to attend with your lawyer).

But, as I said, I think the chances that you will have to appear in court are less than 5%. This number is even less when you are completely honest on all of your filing. So, be completely honest!

N. What Else Will I Have to do to Complete my Bankruptcy Case?

If you have a typical, non-contested bankruptcy filing, your other requirement is to complete a financial management class (this is in addition to the required credit counseling before you file). See the Checklist in Chapter 3 for more information.

O. How Does My Bankruptcy Case End?

In a Chapter 7, the court will enter an order discharging all of the debts for which you are entitled to discharge. Soon thereafter, the Court will enter an order closing your case.

In a Chapter 13 and Chapter 11, you make all your payments under your Chapter 13 bankruptcy plan, then the court will discharge your debts and close your case thereafter.

P. How Will Bankruptcy Affect My Credit Score?

Typically, bankruptcy will reduce your FICO score:

For a 780 credit score – bankruptcy may reduce your credit score up to 240 points.

For a 680 credit score – bankruptcy may reduce your credit score from 100 to 150 points.

But keep in mind a foreclosure typically reduces a credit score by 150 points; repossession has a similar impact on your credit score.

Q. What Happens After My Bankruptcy Case?

You have to make changes to your spending so that you bring in more than you put out. Bankruptcy will give you a fresh start, so that you will be in a position to pay your bills and no longer feel the anxiety you have in the past when the phone rings. Plus, you can start to rebuild your credit as you can make timely payments on debts, since many of your burdensome debts will have been reduced or eliminated through your bankruptcy case.

R. Will Everyone Know About My Bankruptcy Case?

Although filing for bankruptcy commences a public proceeding like any court case, unless you are a celebrity or other prominent person, the only people who will likely know about your bankruptcy filing are those people that you choose to tell.

S. What are the Biggest Advantages in Filing a Bankruptcy Case?

The biggest advantages to filing and completing a bankruptcy case are: the opportunity to make a fresh start without crippling debts; the automatic stay to stop creditors' collection efforts, including foreclosure sales and repossessions; curing defaults on certain secured debts such as your home (in a Chapter 13 bankruptcy case); the discharge of (or greatly reduced payment on) many unsecured debts, including credit card debt; and the ability to challenge debts of creditors which may have violated laws.

T. What are the Biggest Disadvantages in Filing a Bankruptcy Case?

The biggest disadvantages are: you cannot obtain relief on all types of debts, including most mortgages, alimony, child support, most taxes, as well as debts sounding in fraud, and student loans (unless you can show "undue hardship"- a very difficult thing to do); you have a lot of paperwork to complete in order to file and you have to take a hard look at your finances; you cannot file again for bankruptcy for up to 8 years; you could potentially lose some non-exempt property; your credit rating will suffer and you won't be able to make major purchases at a good interest rate for a number of years; and some people may consider a filing for bankruptcy a bad thing or a sort of failure (Don't tell this to Walt Disney, Abraham Lincoln, or Henry Ford. They all filed for bankruptcy and did very well in their lives after their bankruptcy cases!).

U. What Happens in a Chapter 7 Bankruptcy Case?

The three major components of a Chapter 7 bankruptcy case for most debtors in a Chapter 7 bankruptcy case are: credit counseling both before and after filing your bankruptcy case; the preparation and filing of the schedules and other filing documents you must file with the Bankruptcy Court, and your meeting with the Chapter 7 Trustee, normally referred to as a "341 meeting." Chapter 8 of this Guide provides a flow chart of what happens and how to navigate a Chapter 7 bankruptcy case in an easy to read and understand format.

V. What Happens in a Chapter 13 Bankruptcy Case?

The four major components of a Chapter 13 bankruptcy case for most debtors in a Chapter 13 bankruptcy case are: credit counseling both before and after filing your bankruptcy case; the preparation and filing of the schedules, the Chapter 13 plan and other filing documents you must file with the Bankruptcy Court, your meeting with the Chapter 7 Trustee, normally referred to as a "341 meeting," and regular, monthly payments pursuant to your Chapter 13 plan. Chapter 8 of this Guide provides a flow chart of what happens and how to navigate a Chapter 13 bankruptcy case in an easy to read and understand format.

Chapter 2

CAN YOU FILE A CHAPTER 7 BANKRUPTCY CASE?

The biggest, recent change in the Bankruptcy Code is the requirement for passing a "means test" in order to file a Chapter 7 bankruptcy case. Congress made this change in 2005 to cut back on the amount of irresponsible or ill-intentioned bankruptcy cases.

The means test may appear intimidating at first, but I'll walk you through it as far as I can take you. If you are confused or need to continue the test beyond what I explain here, I strongly recommend that you seek the help of a lawyer.

Here's what you need to know to determine whether you can file a Chapter 7 bankruptcy case in California:

In order to file a chapter 7 bankruptcy case in California, you must first determine your current monthly income averaged over the six months prior to your bankruptcy filing. Your current monthly income is defined as your income (plus your spouse's income, if you are filing together) for the six months before filing, plus contributions by others to your household expenses, less Social Security benefits and payments if you are a victim of a war crime or domestic terrorism.

Once you have determined your current monthly income, the first test in determining your eligibility to file a Chapter 7 bankruptcy case is whether your current monthly income exceeds the median income for a family of your size in California.

In 2012, the median amounts are:

1 earner: $47,683 in annual income.

2-person family: $61,539 in annual income.

3-person family: $66,050 in annual income.

4-person family: $74,806 in annual income.

Each Additional Person in Family: add $7,500 in annual income.

If your average income for the last six months does not exceed the median income for your family size in California, then you can choose whether to file a Chapter 7 bankruptcy or a Chapter 13 bankruptcy.

NOTE: If your secured debts (debts backed by a pledge of property) exceed $1,081,400 or your unsecured debts (debts backed solely by your promise to pay) exceed $360,475, you cannot file a Chapter 13 bankruptcy case. You can either file a Chapter 7 bankruptcy case or a Chapter 11 bankruptcy case. You have exceeded the debt limits for a Chapter 13 bankruptcy case.

If Your Income Exceeds Median Income Limits

If your average monthly income exceeds the median amount for a family of your size in California, do not despair. It does not necessarily mean you cannot file a Chapter 7 bankruptcy case.

Instead, it means that you have failed one part of the "means test" and you have more to do. The means test uses a standard mathematical formula to determine whether you can file for Chapter 7 bankruptcy case, or, as set forth in the Bankruptcy Code, whether your filing of a Chapter 7 bankruptcy case would be an "abuse" of the bankruptcy system.

Having failed the first part of the means test, you must then determine whether you can pass the second part. Determining whether you pass the second part of the means test is no easy task. If you fail the first part of the means test because your average income exceeds the median for California and you are still intent on filing a Chapter 7 bankruptcy case, you should consult with a bankruptcy lawyer.

Here's why. Basically, you pass the second part of the means test if your aggregate current monthly income over five years, net of certain statutorily allowed expenses, is more than (i) $11,725, or (ii) 25% of the of your nonpriority unsecured debt, as long as that amount is at least $7,025. Or, more simply, if your current monthly income demonstrates that you can pay your unsecured creditors $11,725 ($195.42 a month) over five years or $7,025 ($117.09 a month) over five years and that is at least 25% of what you currently owe your unsecured creditors, then you cannot file a Chapter 7 bankruptcy case.

You are allowed certain, standard deductions based on the number of vehicles you operate, the number of people in your household and your cost of living. In addition to these standard deductions, you can also deduct the full amount of certain expenses such as your mortgage and loan payments for your car or other vehicle.

As you can see, just the explanation of the second part of the means test is complicated. Do yourself a favor and consult a good bankruptcy attorney if you wish to attempt to pass the second part of the means test. If you fail both parts of the means test, you are presumed to be required to file a Chapter 13 bankruptcy case. There is a presumption of abuse if you file a Chapter 7 bankruptcy case.

However, you can defeat this presumption of abuse by showing special circumstances that justify additional expenses or adjustments of current monthly income. Unless you can overcome the presumption of abuse and you have filed a Chapter 7 bankruptcy case, your bankruptcy case will generally be converted to Chapter 13 (if you consent) or the case will be dismissed. A bankruptcy lawyer is the best person to assist you in defeating the presumption based on special circumstances.

EXCEPTIONS TO THE MEANS TEST:

If you are a veteran, and you are disabled, and your indebtedness occurred primarily during a period in which you were: on active duty, or performing a homeland defense activity, you are exempt from the means test.

If you are a member of a reserve component of the Armed Forces and members of the National Guard and you were called to active duty after September 11, 2001, for a period of at least 90 days or you have performed homeland defense activity for a period of at least 90 days, you are excluded from all forms of means testing during the time of active duty or homeland defense activity and for 540 days thereafter.

NOTE: If your secured debts (debts backed by a pledge of property) exceed $1,081,400 or your unsecured debts (debts backed solely by your promise to pay) exceed $360,475, you cannot file a Chapter 13 bankruptcy case. You will have to file a Chapter 11 bankruptcy case unless you can defeat the presumption as set forth above and could then either file a Chapter 7 bankruptcy case or a Chapter 11 bankruptcy case.

Chapter 3

CHECKLIST FOR FILING YOUR BANKRUPTCY CASE

Before, during and after your bankruptcy case, you can use the following checklist to ensure that you have considered and done everything you would likely need to do in your case.

This is your Bankruptcy Checklist for a Successful Bankruptcy Case:

Part I: What You Need to Do Pre-Filing

Complete Credit Counseling Briefing

Before filing a bankruptcy petition under any chapter, you must obtain a briefing by a credit counseling agency approved by the United States trustee or the Bankruptcy Administrator. The briefing must be obtained within 180 days before commencement of your case, and a certificate of proof of completion must be filed with the court. The cost of the briefing is about $50, and it can be completed online, by telephone or in person. The bankruptcy court can excuse you from the requirement if you are physically or mentally disabled or on active military duty. Also, the court can approve a delay in obtaining the briefing if there are exigent circumstances preventing you from obtaining the counseling before filing the petition, but these are difficult to obtain.

Pay Filing Fees

Bankruptcy petitions must be accompanied by a filing and administrative fee payable to the court. Currently the fees for bankruptcy cases are: $306 for Chapter 7 cases; $281 for Chapter 13 and 12 cases and $1,046 for Chapter 11 cases. Filing and administrative fees are in addition to attorney fees and counseling fees. You may file an application to pay the filing fees in installments, and courts usually allow payment over time, in four to five segments. In a Chapter 7 case, the bankruptcy court may approve a waiver of the filing fee upon application that conforms to Official Form 3B and proof that your income is less than 150 percent of the official poverty line based on the size of your family.

150% Poverty guidelines for 2012:

1 person in the family: $1,396.25 in monthly income; $16,755.00 in yearly income.

2 people in the family: $1,891.25 in monthly income; $22,695.00 in yearly income.

3 people in the family: $2,386.25 in monthly income; $28,635.00 in yearly income.

4 people in the family: $2,881.25 in monthly income; $34,575.00 in yearly income.

5 people in the family: $3,376.25 in monthly income; $40,515.00 in yearly income.

6 people in the family: $3,871.25 in monthly income; $46,455.00 in yearly income.

7 people in the family: $4,366.25 in monthly income; $52,395.00 in yearly income.

8 people in the family: $4,861.25 in monthly income; $58,335.00 in yearly income.

Each Additional Person add: $495.00 in monthly income; $5,940.00 in yearly income.

Part II: What You Need to Do For Filing

Submit Filing Documents to Bankruptcy Court

You must file certain documents to commence your bankruptcy case. If these required documents are not filed, the court will dismiss the case and you will lose the benefits of bankruptcy protection.

To commence a case, the debtor must file the following documents:

A. Official Form 1: the voluntary petition

B. Official Form 21: the statement of Social Security number. The Social Security statement must contain your full number. Pursuant to the privacy policy of the United States Courts, the full Social Security number does not become a public record, and only creditors will receive the full number to enable them to identify the debtor in their records.

C. A list of creditors' names and addresses: The list of creditors, often known as the "mailing matrix," is not an official form, but is often the subject of a local form.

D. A certificate from an approved credit counseling agency that the debtor had the required briefing

At the same time or shortly after a case begins, you must file:

E. Official Form 7: Schedules of assets, liabilities, income and expenses. These include the following schedules:

Real Property (Schedule A);
Personal Property (Schedule B);
Property Claimed as Exempt (Schedule C);
Creditors Holding Secured Claims (Schedule D);
Creditors Holding Unsecured Priority Claims (Schedule E);
Creditors Holding Unsecured Nonpriority Claims (Schedule F);

Executory Contracts and Unexpired Leases (Schedule G); and

Co-debtors (Schedule H).

F. Official Form 7, cont'd: Statement of Financial Affairs.

G. Form 22A, B, or C: the "means test" calculation (depending on your bankruptcy Chapter).

H. Form B203: the attorney's disclosure of compensation.

I. (Chapter 7 cases only)- Official Form 8: a statement of intention with respect to secured debts.

J. (Chapter 13 cases only)- Chapter 13 plan: No official form exists for the Chapter 13 plan, but many jurisdictions have a form of Chapter 13 plan that is required or suggested. A model Chapter 13 bankruptcy plan is attached below.

K. Certain Court Specific Local Forms and Other Forms. Check with the Bankruptcy Court where you are filing to see if you need to file any local forms in addition to documents listed above. Also, review SectionVI of this Chapter for forms that if you fail to file will get your case dimissed.

Many of the required documents must be signed by you under the pain and penalty of perjury. If you make false statements on the forms, or omit information that makes the forms misleading, the consequences may be severe, including denial of your bankruptcy discharge or criminal prosecution. Make sure all forms are accurate and complete, and if mistakes are discovered, the documents should be promptly amended. These filing documents are usually due within 15 days after the petition date. If these documents are not filed, the court will issue an order to file the documents. You may obtain an extension of time for filing the documents, but you must request before the deadline. Bankruptcy courts typically will dismiss your bankruptcy case if you do not file on time.

The California bankruptcy courts cannot supply these forms. These forms are available from office supply stores, legal stationary stores and can be accessed for printing from the Federal Judiciary's web site at http://www.uscourts.gov/bkforms/bankruptcy_forms.html#official.

File Payment Advices or Proof of Income

You must file copies of all "payment advices" with the bankruptcy court or submit them to the trustee. "Payment advices" are evidence of salary or income earned within 60 days before the commencement of the case. Some courts require that the documents be filed with the court, whereas others require that they be submitted to the trustee before the meeting of creditors (the "Section 341" meeting).

Part III: What You Need to Do During Your Bankruptcy Case

Produce Tax Returns

You must produce tax returns to the trustee, and to creditors upon request. The federal income tax return or an IRS tax transcript for the most recent tax year before the filing of your petition must be given to the trustee at least a week before the meeting of creditors. However, if you were not required to file a return, for example, because you had insufficient gross income under the IRS rules, a return need not be provided. If you do not have a return, a transcript can be obtained from the IRS and submitted to the trustee instead of a return. If you fail to provide a tax return or transcript to the IRS, the bankruptcy court may dismiss the bankruptcy case.

Don't have your most recent tax return? You can easily get your federal tax return transcript for free by calling 1-800-829-1040, or by mailing or faxing IRS Form 4506T to the IRS. See www.irs.gov for more information.

Attend Meeting of the Creditors

After your bankruptcy case is commenced, you will receive notice of the meeting of creditors, which is commonly referred to as the Section 341 meeting, after the Bankruptcy Code section requiring the meeting. You must attend this meeting in person. You will be administered an oath by the trustee, and the trustee will ask you questions about your assets, liabilities, income and expenses under oath and the proceeding is recorded. The purpose of the trustee's questions is to ascertain whether you have made a complete and accurate list of your assets and liabilities and whether you have any assets that can be liquidated for distribution to creditors.

The Section 341 meeting is recorded and is held in a public place, usually with other debtors present. Creditors may attend the meeting. However, creditors are not required to attend and usually do not attend. The trustee will usually examine you for five to ten minutes, but may continue the meeting on another date if there is insufficient time and the examination is not concluded. You are required to bring a picture form of identification, proof of Social Security number, recent bank account statements and proof of current income, such as a pay stub. Some trustees will send you a letter requesting that additional documents be brought to the Section 341 meeting. It is in your best interest to satisfy all of the trustee's requests to the best of your ability. If you do not speak English, an interpreter may be provided for the Section 341 meeting.

Bankruptcy Court Appearance?

Most debtors never see the inside of a bankruptcy courtroom. The Section 341 meeting is usually the only event that you will have to attend in person.

Complete Personal Financial Management Course

You must complete a personal financial management course after the commencement of your bankruptcy case and file a certificate of completion of the course. The course must be given by an instructor approved by the United States trustee program. In a Chapter 7 case, the certificate must be filed within 45 days after the Section 341 meeting, and in a Chapter 13 case, by the last plan payment. The cost of the instruction varies, but generally does not cost more than $100. You may ask the court for a waiver of the course requirement on the grounds that you are mentally or physically disabled, or are on active military duty.

Part IV: What You Need to Do to End Your Bankruptcy Case

Getting Your Bankruptcy Discharge

Once you have performed your required duties, your bankruptcy discharge will routinely take place unless a creditor or the trustee files an adversary proceeding against you seeking to exempt a debt from discharge or denying your bankruptcy discharge. Make sure that you receive notice from the court that your bankruptcy case is discharged and closed soon thereafter.

Part V: What About Getting Help for Your Bankruptcy Case

Seek Legal Advice?

You may be wondering whether you should file the bankruptcy case with or without an attorney. The rules and standards you must adhere to are the same whether you have a lawyer or not. You will have to comply with the requirements of the Bankruptcy Code and the Rules. You must properly file your bankruptcy case and handle it properly throughout the case.

Bankruptcy is complicated. Understanding bankruptcy law and bankruptcy rules is often beyond the ability of a person not educated in the law and even many lawyers who do not regularly practice bankruptcy law. The legal rights available to you under your personal situation will vary. The consequences of making mistakes in a bankruptcy case can be drastic.

Just think about it this way, you may know something about electricity, but would you really want to rewire your whole house by yourself?

Paying for an Attorney

Ironically, most debtors need to save money to file a bankruptcy case with a lawyer. Attorneys generally charge an up-front cash fee or a combination of an up-front fee with your balance to be paid over time. Remember that you must also pay a filing fee with your bankruptcy petition, unless the court waives the fee or allows it to be paid in installments. If you simply cannot pay, pro bono programs and agencies provide free legal services to debtors. Lawyers have a professional duty to provide legal services to those who are unable to pay.

Professional Help?

People plagued by financial troubles aren't always in the state of mind to make the best decisions about their financial condition. Whether or not you plan on working with an attorney, you should likely seek advice from a competent professional about whether or not to file for bankruptcy. Consumer bankruptcy lawyers will often provide a consultation to prospective clients for little or no fee. Seek a consultation before you embark on a bankruptcy case to determine if there are less drastic alternatives that could work for you.

As set forth in this guide, there are many reasons to stay out of a bankruptcy case, *and* there are reasons to choose to file. If you choose to file, there are further issues as to the appropriate chapter for relief and the timing of a bankruptcy filing, as well as technical requirements affecting your rights. These decisions are extremely complicated and require an evaluation of the facts of a particular case and an assessment of the applicable law. Good representation by a qualified professional may be critical.

WARNING: BANKRUPTCY PETITION PREPARERS:

Be alert when dealing with petition preparers. The role of non-attorney petition preparers is solely to type information on official bankruptcy forms. Petition preparers are barred by law from providing legal advice – they cannot explain how to answer legal questions or assist in bankruptcy court. Petition preparers must sign all documents they prepare, print their name, address, and Social Security number on such documents, and furnish copies to the debtor. They cannot sign a document on the debtor's behalf or receive payment from the debtor for court fees.

Part VI: Easiest Ways to Have Your Bankruptcy Case Dismissed

Your bankruptcy case will likely be dismissed if you do not file these forms as required by the Bankruptcy Court. You may get a reminder or warning from the Bankruptcy Court but you cannot rely on any leeway so comply from the beginning. You risk dismissal if you do not file:

A.   **Filing fee of $281 (Chapter 13) or $306 (Chapter 7).** You may ask the Bankruptcy Court for permission to pay the fee in installments by filing a signed application for Court approval.

B.   **Voluntary Petition (Official Form 1).**

C.   **Certificate of Credit Counseling.** (Or § 109(h)(3) certification or § 109(h)(4) request). Must be filed **WITH** the petition. Fed.R.Bankr.P. 1007(b) & (c).

D.   **Statement of Social Security Number (Official Form 21).** Must be filed **WITH** the petition.

E.   **Names and addresses of all creditors of the debtor ("Creditor Matrix").**

F.   **Notice to Individual Debtor with Primarily Consumer Debts under 11 U.S.C. § 342(b)**, if applicable. Must be filed with the petition or within 14 days.

G.   **Statement of current monthly income (Official Form 22C).** Must be filed with the petition or within 14 days. Rule 1007, Fed.R.Bankr.P. (In order to prepare Part I of this form, each person filing will need to have copies of their pay stubs or other evidence of income for the six (6) month period preceding the bankruptcy filing)

H.   **Schedules of assets and liabilities (Official Form 6).** Must be filed with the petition or within 14 days.

I.   **Schedule of executory contracts and unexpired leases (Schedule G of Official Form 6).** Must be filed with the petition or within 14 days.

J.   **Schedules of current income and expenditures (Schedules I and J of Official Form 6).** Must be filed with the petition or within 14 days.

K. **Statement of financial affairs (Official Form 7).** Must be filed with the petition or within 14 days.

L. **Copies of all pay stubs or other evidence of income received by the debtor within 60 days before the filing of the petition.** To be provided to the Chapter 7 or 13 Trustee no later than 7 days before the first meeting of creditors.

M. **Copies of the most recently filed tax returns.** To be provided to the Chapter 7 or Chapter 13 Trustee no later than 7 days before the first meeting of creditors.

N. **<u>You must appear at the first meeting of creditors (the 341 meeting) or your case may be dismissed</u>.**

<u>For Chapter 13 the following are also required:</u>

O. **Independent evidence of valuation, copies of deeds, Declaration of Homestead, and insurance binders for all real estate.** To be provided to the Chapter 13 Trustee on or before the first meeting of creditors.

P. **Chapter 13 Plan.** Must be filed with the petition or within 14 days thereafter. Fed.R.Bankr.P. 3015.

Chapter 4

BASICS OF BANKRUPTCY

The Constitution of the United States gave the United States Congress the right to make laws regarding bankruptcy. Using this ability, Congress has enacted federal laws and enabled regulations that have resulted in today's Bankruptcy system. There are 94 Bankruptcy jurisdictions in which a Bankruptcy court is located.

Bankruptcy is a legal procedure which allows individuals and businesses to obtain relief from debts. This relief from debts enables individuals and businesses to have a fresh start in their financial burdens. Bankruptcy may also remedy financial injustices.

You commence your bankruptcy case by filing your bankruptcy petition, one of the official bankruptcy documents discussed in the Checklist in Chapter 3. Filing your bankruptcy petition will give you an immediate break from collection efforts of creditors- this is called the "automatic stay.". When you successfully complete your bankruptcy case, you may have many of your debts discharged by order of the bankruptcy court. You will be released from your obligation to repay those debts that are discharged.

Overview of the Process

Bankruptcy provides numerous protections and benefits, but follows well-established rules and laws that dictate what happens to you and your property. Follow the flow charts in Chapter 8 to see the step that you have to follow, explained in greater detail in the Checklist.

The Automatic Stay

The moment you commence your bankruptcy case, an order of the bankruptcy court called the automatic stay goes into effect. This requires cessation of all collection actions, lawsuits in which you are a defendant, foreclosures, wage garnishments, evictions, demands for repayment of debts and phone calls to collect debts. If a creditor takes action in violation of the stay, you may recover actual and punitive damages as well as attorneys' fees from the creditor.

The automatic stay is not unlimited. Congress has declared 28 exceptions to the automatic stay, including fines from the prosecution of criminal actions and the collection of alimony and child support. The bankruptcy court may grant a creditor relief from the automatic stay upon the filing of a motion in which the creditor gives the bankruptcy court good cause to lift the automatic stay as to its debt. Other limitations on the automatic stay arise, especially where the debtor has had one or more prior bankruptcy cases which were dismissed within a year of the current filing. There are special provisions that apply to eviction cases which give landlords and debtors specific rights and obligations.

What Happens to Your Property Upon Filing?

When you commence your bankruptcy case, all your legal and equitable interests, including interests in real and personal property, become property of the bankruptcy estate. The trustee of the bankruptcy case will then administer all of the property for the benefit of your creditors.

Bankruptcy law entitles you to claim certain property as "exempt." You keep your exempt property and it stays out of the hands of your creditors. Some state law exemptions have been in effect for hundreds of years and are outdated, such as exemptions for church pews, the family Bible, two swine and four tons of hay.

Property which you are typically allowed to exempt includes:

Some or all of the equity in a debtor's personal residence

Some or all of the value in a vehicle

A debtor's tools of the trade

Household goods

Jewelry

Life insurance

Personal injury claims

The list of exemptions available under the federal exemption scheme is more current and provides categories of exempt property with values that are adjusted for the cost of living every three years. In the event a creditor has a court ordered lien which impairs an exemption, you may request that the creditor's lien be "avoided." When a court avoids a creditor's lien, it removes it from securing the property and the judicial lien will be released. This ability to avoid liens is especially relevant regarding your homestead exemption. If any voluntary mortgages and/or your homestead exemption exceed the value of your home, you can seek to avoid any judgment liens attached to your house. Your specific exemptions are listed in full in Chapter 9.

Alaska, Arizona, California, Idaho, Louisiana, Nevada, New Mexico, Puerto Rico, Texas, Washington and Wisconsin are generally considered community property states, so you want to use extra caution if you are married and filing for bankruptcy in one of these without your spouse. Debts are generally considered to be debts of both spouses, even if the debt was taken out only in one spouse's name.

The Bankruptcy Discharge

The United States Supreme Court has emphasized that bankruptcy *"gives to the honest but unfortunate debtor…a new opportunity in life and a clear field for future effort, unhampered by the pressure and discouragement of preexisting debt."*

The discharge order of the bankruptcy court releases you from personal liability for debts. Discharge provides a permanent injunction preventing collection of all of the debts to which it applies. After a discharge, you enjoy your property (other than property of the estate) free from the claims of creditors. The best example of property that is free from the creditors after discharge is future earnings.

However, the discharge does not apply to all of your debts. Automatic exceptions set forth in the Bankruptcy Code, such as most taxes, alimony, spousal and child support, criminal restitution and fines, and student loans where the debtor does not prove repayment is an undue hardship will not be discharged. Moreover, a creditor can bring a proceeding within a bankruptcy case (known as an adversary proceeding) to determine that a debt should not be discharged if the debt was incurred by fraud, willful and malicious injury, and other like causes. The bankruptcy court may determine after litigation that a debt will not be discharged or is "nondischargeable." If you commit certain offenses, such as not disclosing all of your assets or making a false oath in your bankruptcy case, the bankruptcy court may deny discharge of all of your debts.

There are six types of bankruptcy relief and each type is called a chapter for its section in the bankruptcy legislation. The two types most common for individuals are Chapter 7 and Chapter 13 bankruptcy cases. Chapter 11 is generally used by individuals with very large debts and those who have unincorporated businesses in their names.

Chapter 5

CHAPTER 7 BANKRUPTCY CASES

Chapter 7 is the bankruptcy chapter most people think of when they refer to bankruptcy.

A Chapter 7 bankruptcy case is a liquidation of both your debts and your assets under the supervision of a trustee. More often than not, Chapter 7 cases are routine. The vast majority of Chapter 7 debtors find that their cases are "discharged" (or released) and then closed without any of their assets being liquidated or distributed to any creditors. In a majority of Chapter 7 cases, the debtors never appear in front of the bankruptcy judge, but only attend a meeting of creditors conducted by a trustee.

When you file a Chapter 7 case, your bankruptcy case is controlled by a Chapter 7 trustee appointed by the United States Trustee Office (a division of the Department of Justice). In a Chapter 7 case, the trustee investigates your assets, determines whether to object to any exemptions you have claimed (state and federal laws protect certain property), and has the ability to sell any assets that are not exempt and distribute the proceeds of the sales to creditors. The trustee also has the ability to object to creditors' claims.

To qualify for relief in Chapter 7, you must meet the eligibility criteria by obtaining prepetition credit counseling briefing, and as discussed in Chapter 2, by completing the means test. You must file a schedule of assets, including claims of your exemptions and liabilities, and pay the filing fee unless excused by the bankruptcy court.

Unless a creditor, the trustee or another interested party files an objection, the court will enter a discharge. The discharge of a debtor in a Chapter 7 case may not affect certain debts like your mortgage or auto loan, because you have pledged your property to obtain the debt and other debts that Congress has excluded from the bankruptcy discharge, such as student loans, alimony, child support, and many taxes (see Chapter 11 for more about these "non-dischargeable"debts).

You can enter into reaffirmation agreements for the purpose of retaining your secured collateral, such as your house or car (more on this option below).

You will not receive a discharge of debts excepted from the discharge under the Code, or if the bankruptcy court carves out a particular debt from your discharge after litigation. Moreover, you can be denied a bankruptcy discharge if you are found to have lied to the trustee or court, fraudulently transferred property, or destroyed records. In addition, the discharge can be revoked if it was obtained through fraud.

Chapter 6

CHAPTER 13 BANKRUPTCY CASES

Chapter 13 of the Bankruptcy Code is entitled "Debt Adjustments for Individuals with Regular Income." Unlike in a Chapter 7 case, in a Chapter 13 bankruptcy case you file a plan under which you propose to pay all or a percentage of your debt over a period of three to five years, depending on the your income. The primary debtors in Chapter 13 bankruptcy cases are people in default on their mortgages who want to stay in their home, and people who have nonexempt assets they want to keep and debts that they need to pay over time.

Advantages and Disadvantages of Chapter 13 Bankruptcy Cases

Several important reasons may persuade you to choose Chapter 13. Most importantly, in Chapter 13, you can retain all your property while performing under the Chapter 13 plan. Thus, if you have property not covered by exemptions under state or federal law (non-exempt property) that you want to retain, Chapter 13 may be your best option. A self-employed individual who operates a non-incorporated business may continue to operate the business and include the business's debts in the Chapter 13 plan. Moreover, since defaults in home mortgages can be paid over the term of the plan, you may be able to save your home from foreclosure in a Chapter 13. You can reduce certain mortgages and liens to the value of the property (such as on a second home or rental property) and pay them over the term of your Chapter 13 plan.

Judicial liens on real estate which impair your exemptions (such as your homestead exemption) can be avoided and re-characterized as unsecured claims. Furthermore, you can pay prepetition tax claims with legal priority over the term of the plan. One of the most significant advantages of Chapter 13 is that, in addition to the automatic stay for you as the debtor, a co-debtor stay extends to individuals who are also liable with you on consumer debts throughout the term of the Chapter 13 plan.

Some disadvantages exist in a Chapter 13 plan. First, during the years that you are paying debts under the plan, you are under the jurisdiction of the bankruptcy court. Not only does the bankruptcy court scrutinize your financial life, but your finances are subject to monitoring by the Chapter 13 trustee and creditors. If you fail to make a payment under the plan, the trustee and creditors can seek to dismiss your Chapter 13 case resulting in the lost opportunity for a discharge.

In addition, if during the term of the plan your income or assets increase, those parties can request that the plan be modified to increase payments. Moreover, Chapter 13 cases are more costly than Chapter 7. You must pay a trustee's commission - approximately 10 percent of the plan disbursements. Your attorneys' fees are higher for Chapter 13 cases than Chapter 7 cases, usually ranging from $ 2,500 to $ 3,500, plus filing fees, depending on the jurisdiction. Attorneys' fees for a Chapter 7 range between $1,000 and $1,500.

The Chapter 13 Plan and Plan Confirmation

As a Chapter 13 debtor, you must file a plan that properly treats the debts owed by the debtor according to the legal priority of creditors' claims. Priority claims, such as taxes, must be paid in full over the term of the plan. A plan can cure a default in a mortgage or lease by paying the amount in arrears over the plan term, while maintaining regular payments. Although home mortgages cannot be modified under a Chapter 13 plan, and vehicle purchase loans obtained within 910 days prior to commencement of the case must also be paid in full, some types of secured claims can be modified and the debtor need only pay the value of the collateral, plus market interest rate over the term of the plan.

The plan need not pay unsecured claims in full as long it provides that the debtor will pay all projected "disposable income" over an "applicable commitment period," and as long as unsecured creditors receive at least as much under the plan as they would receive under Chapter 7. In Chapter 13, "disposable income" is defined as income (other than child support payments received by the debtor) less amounts reasonably necessary for the maintenance or support of the debtor or dependents and less charitable contributions up to 15% of the debtor's gross income. If you operate a business, the definition of disposable income excludes those amounts which are necessary for ordinary operating expenses.

The "applicable commitment period" refers to the required duration of the plan, and it depends on your current monthly income. The applicable commitment period must be three years if your current monthly income is less than the state median for a family of the same size - and five years if the current monthly income is greater than a family of the same size. The plan can be a period shorter than the applicable commitment period if the debtor proposes to pay unsecured debts in full.

The trustee and creditors have the right to object to your Chapter 13 plan.

The discharge in your Chapter 13 bankruptcy case releases you from all debts provided for by the plan or disallowed, subject to certain exceptions. The discharge provides an injunction that prevents creditors provided for in the Chapter 13 plan from pursuing you on the discharged obligations. Exceptions from discharge include certain long-term obligations (such as a home mortgage), debts for alimony or child support, certain taxes, debts for most government-funded or guaranteed educational loans or benefit overpayments, debts arising from death or personal injury caused by driving while intoxicated or under the influence of drugs, and debts for restitution or a criminal fine included in a sentence on the debtor's conviction of a crime.

Chapter 7

CHAPTER 11 BANKRUPTCY CASES

Most individuals don't need to worry about a Chapter 11 bankruptcy case. After all, unless you have a business in your name, you should likely strive to save yourself money and seek bankruptcy relief under Chapter 13. You should look to Chapter 11 if your debt exceeds the Chapter 13 debt limits. These limits in 2012 are: $360,475 in unsecured debts and $1,081,400 in secured debts.

An individual Chapter 11 case closely resembles a Chapter 13 case because debtors must devote their property and projected disposable income acquired after beginning of their case to the repayment of creditors for five years. The bankruptcy court does not grant debtors in a Chapter 11 cases a discharge of their debt until they complete their Chapter 11 bankruptcy plan.

The typical Chapter 11 bankruptcy cases allow debtors to continue to operate their businesses or oversee their lives and to stay in control of all of their assets while they restructure their finances.

While in Chapter 11, you can use the collateral of your secured lender and even borrow money to operate or exist in exiting Chapter 11. Unless the court appoints a trustee, during the first 120 days of a Chapter 11 case, only you have the exclusive right to file a Chapter 11 bankruptcy plan.

The Chapter 11 bankruptcy plan determines how much creditors will be paid and when they will be paid. The plan must classify claims according to their legal priority. Along with the plan, you must file a disclosure statement providing adequate information to creditors to enable them to decide whether to accept or reject the plan. The disclosure statement should describe your financial problems, assets, liabilities, treatment of creditors under the plan, alternatives to the plan and the feasibility of the plan. The bankruptcy court will determine if the disclosure statement has sufficient information so that the plan can be circulated for voting.

Creditors are placed in "classes" according to the type of debt they are owed and other legal rights. The plan provides how the debtor will pay each class of creditors. Any class of claims that has its legal rights altered by the plan is considered "impaired." If a class of claims is not impaired under the plan, that class is deemed to have accepted the plan. If a class is impaired, however, that class of claims votes on the plan.

As a Chapter 11 debtor, you must demonstrate that the plan is in the best interest of creditors, meaning that under the plan, creditors receive as much as they would if the debtor had filed a Chapter 7 liquidation case. You must also show that the plan is feasible, meaning that you will not likely need further reorganization after the court confirms the plan. Finally, if a class of claims votes to reject the plan, the bankruptcy court can still confirm the plan if you can show that the plan does not discriminate unfairly against the rejecting class and that the plan is fair and equitable as to the rejecting class.

Under a Chapter 11 plan, you may obtain a "cram down" or modification of secured claims by restructuring the debt and paying the value of the collateral over time at a present value rate of interest, but this does not include the mortgage on your primary residence. The bankruptcy court will hold a confirmation hearing and determine whether to approve the plan. For individuals, you do not obtain a discharge until plan payment is complete.

Chapter 8

FLOW CHARTS OF TYPICAL BANKRUPTCY CASES

The following two charts walk you through the potential steps involved in a typical Chapter 7 bankruptcy case and a typical Chapter 13 bankruptcy case:

Typical Chapter 7 Bankruptcy

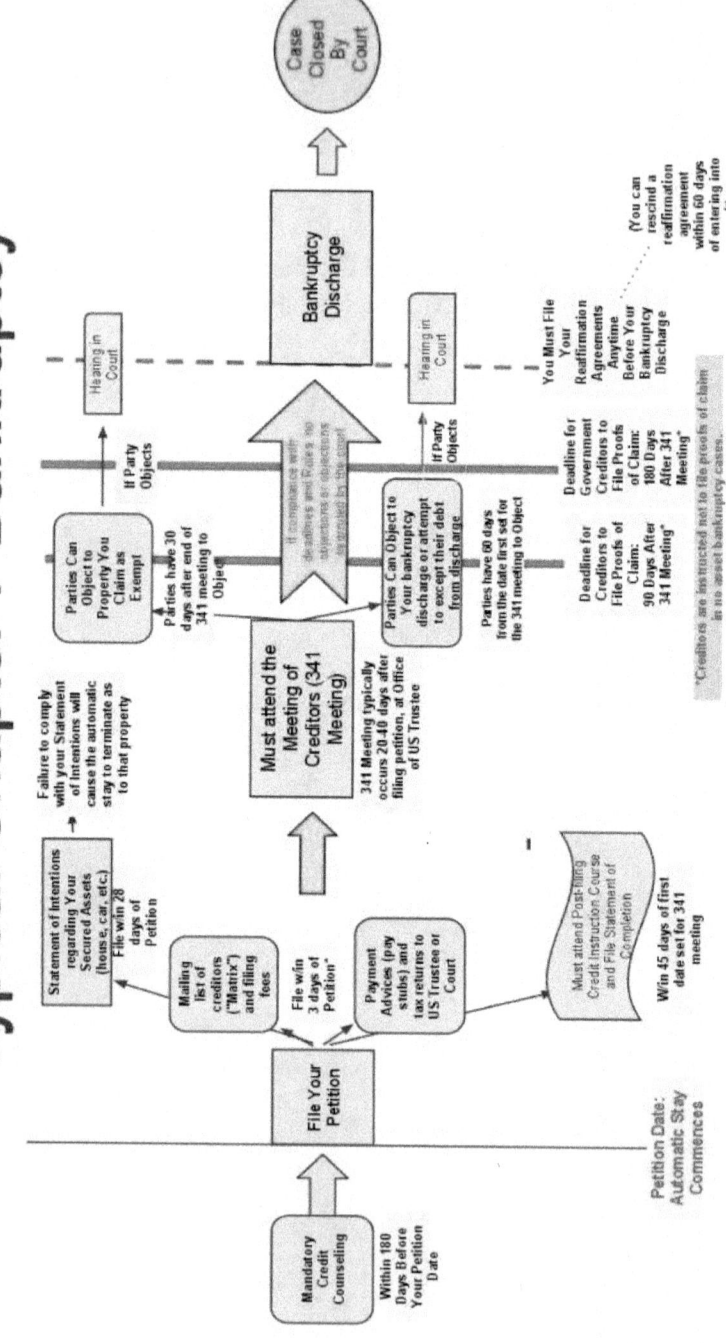

Case Closed By Court

Bankruptcy Discharge

Hearing in Court

Hearing in Court

Parties Can Object to Property You Claim as Exempt

Parties have 30 days after end of 341 meeting to Object

Parties Can Object to Your bankruptcy discharge or attempt to except their debt from discharge

Parties have 60 days from the date first set for the 341 meeting to Object

If Party Objects

If Party Objects

If comply with all the deadlines and Rules no objections & objections as granted by the court

Statement of Intentions regarding Your Secured Assets (house, car, etc.)
File w/in 28 days of Petition

Failure to comply with your Statement of Intentions will cause the automatic stay to terminate as to that property

Must attend the Meeting of Creditors (341 Meeting)

341 Meeting typically occurs 20-40 days after filing petition, at Office of US Trustee

You Must File Your Reaffirmation Agreements Anytime Before Your Bankruptcy Discharge

(You can rescind a reaffirmation agreement within 60 days of entering into it)

Deadline for Creditors to File Proofs of Claim: 90 Days After 341 Meeting*

Deadline for Government Creditors to File Proofs of Claim: 180 Days After 341 Meeting*

*Creditors are instructed not to file proofs of claim in no asset bankruptcy cases.

Mailing list of creditors ("Matrix") and filing fees

File w/in 3 days of Petition*

Payment Advices (pay stubs) and tax returns to US Trustee or Court

Must attend Post-filing Credit Instruction Course and File Statement of Completion

W/in 45 days of first date set for 341 meeting

File Your Petition

Mandatory Credit Counseling

Within 180 Days Before Your Petition Date

Petition Date: Automatic Stay Commences

Typical Chapter 13 Bankruptcy

Mandatory Credit Counseling
Within 180 Days Before Your Petition Date

File Your Petition

Petition Date: Automatic Stay Commences

Statement of Intentions regarding Your Secured Assets (house, car, etc.)
File w/in 28 days of Petition

Failure to comply with your Statement of Intentions will cause the automatic stay to terminate as to that property

Mailing list of creditors ("Matrix") and filing fees
File w/in 3 days of Petition"

Payment Advices (pay stubs) and tax returns to US Trustee or Court

Must attend Post-Filing Credit Instruction Course and File Statement of Completion
W/in 45 days of first date set for 341 meeting

Chapter 13 Plan

Must attend the Meeting of Creditors (341 Meeting)
341 Meeting typically occurs 20-40 days after filing petition, at Office of US Trustee

Parties Can Object to Property You Claim as Exempt
Parties have 30 days after end of 341 meeting to Object

If Party Objects

Hearing in Court

If compliance with deadlines and Rules, no objections overruled by the court, and all plan payments are made

Bankruptcy Discharge

Case Closed By Court

Deadline for Creditors to File Proofs of Claim:
90 Days After 341 Meeting"

Deadline for Creditors to File Proofs of Claim:
90 Days After 341 Meeting"

Parties Can Object to your Plan

If Party Objects

Hearing in Court

Plan allowed by Court or no objections then....

3 to 5 Years of Plan Payments

Chapter 9

WHAT EXEMPTIONS ARE AVAILABLE TO YOU?

As discussed, exemptions are assets that are not included in your bankruptcy estate and therefore are not available to creditors to satisfy their debts. Bankruptcy law allowed each state to choose whether to make federal exemptions set forth in the Bankruptcy Code available to residents in its state in addition to its state law exemptions, or to "opt out" and allow its residents to only choose state law exemptions.

Do not rely on the following exemption summary absolutely. It gives you a good idea but, because exemptions are constantly fluctuating, the amounts and terms may not be precise for the time you are filing. Be sure you double-check or ask an attorney about when and how you have to claim your exemptions in order for them to be valid in your bankruptcy case. Exemptions and the amounts of the exemptions in particular change at irregular times, so be sure to check with your local laws, a local lawyer or the website www.legalconsumer.com provides updated exemptions as well. The following exemptions are current as of the fall of 2011.

Although California has "opted out" and does not allow you to choose between state and federal exemptions, California allows you to choose between **two different sets of exemptions** under its state laws. Choosing between the two California alternatives is limited as follows

1. You and your spouse filing jointly must both elect the same alternative;

2. If you are debtor filing individually, you cannot elect the second set of exemptions set forth below unless your nonfiling spouse agrees to waive the right to claim these exemptions if he or she files a subsequent bankruptcy case. Cal. Civ. Proc. Code § 703.140(a); and

3. If you are not married, you may select either set of exemptions, but not both.

ALTERNATIVE I:

The exemptions available to you under the first set California state law are generally as follows (the statute is more complex that as set forth below but this summary should give you a general idea):

Homestead Exemption.

You can take the following exemption for your homestead (your home and adjacent land):

Your interests in real or personal property you occupy including mobile home, boat, stock cooperative, community apartment, planned development, or condo to $75,000 if single & not disabled; $100,000 for families if no other member has a homestead (if only one spouse files, may exempt one-half of amount if home held as community property and all of amount if home held as tenants in common); $175,000 if 65 or older, or physically or mentally disabled; $175,000 if 55 or older, single, & with gross annual income under $15,000 or married & gross annual income under $20,000 & creditors seek to force the sale of your home; forced sale proceeds received exempt for 6 months after; separated but married debtor may claim homestead in community property still occupied by other spouse. (Husband & wife may not double). Cal. Civ. Proc. Code §§ 704.720, 704.730

Personal Property.

You can exempt the following personal property:

1. Household furniture, appliances, provisions, wearing apparel and other personal effects ordinarily and reasonably necessary to you and dependents and used at the principal place of residence. Cal. Civ. Proc. Code § 704.020(a)(1).

2. Material to be used to repair or improve a residence when your equity in the material does not exceed $2,875. Cal. Civ. Proc. Code § 704.030.

3. Jewelry, heirlooms, and works of art not to exceed $7,175. Cal. Civ. Proc. Code § 704.040.

4. Health aid reasonably necessary for you or dependent to work or sustain health are fully exempt. Cal. Civ. Proc. Code § 704.050.

5. Tools, implements, instruments, materials, uniforms, furnishings, books, equipment, one commercial motor vehicle, one vessel, and other personal property are exempt to the extent that the aggregate equity does not exceed $7,175 per debtor or spouse in earning and livelihood or $14,350 in the exercise of the same trade, business or profession by which both earn a livelihood. Cal. Civ. Proc. Code § 704.060(a). For a commercial vehicle to be exempt, there must not be a claim for an exemption of a personal vehicle which is reasonably adequate for use in the trade, business or profession. Cal. Civ. Proc. Code § 704.060(c). The exemption for a commercial vehicle is limited to $4,850 ($9,700 if used by debtor and spouse). Cal. Civ. Proc. Code § 704.060 (d).

6. Motor vehicles in which there is an aggregate equity of

$2,725. Cal. Civ. Proc. Code § 704.010.

7. There is an absolute exemption for a family burial plot. The cemetery plot for you and spouse is exempt if you claim the exemption. Cal. Civ. Proc. Code § 704.200(b) and (c).

8. There is an absolute exemption for deposit accounts that are designated payees of directly deposited public benefit payments in the amount of $1,425 for one depositor and $2,150 for two or more depositors unless the deposit represents a benefit to only one depositor in which case the amount is $1,425. The exemption is $2,875 for single depositors and $4,300 for two or more depositors when the depositors are the designated payees of directly deposited social security payments. Cal. Civ. Proc. Code § 704.080(b).

Pay and Wages.

Your wages are exempt as follows:

Seventy-five percent of paid earnings. Cal. Civ. Proc. Code § 704.070(b)(2).

Benefits and Insurance.

You can exempt the following benefits and insurance:

1. There is an absolute exemption for all rights and benefits under a public retirement system. Cal. Civ. Proc. Code § 704.110(b).

2. There is an absolute exemption for all vacation credit of public employees. Cal. Civ. Proc. Code § 704.113(b).

3. All amounts for distribution by private retirement plan

such as a union retirement plan, profit sharing plan or self-employed retirement plan are exempt. Cal. Civ. Proc. Code § 704.115(b).

4. Amounts held for payment for unemployment compensation benefits, disability benefits, extended duration benefits, funeral, benefits under a plan established by an employer, unemployment benefits by a fraternal organization, and benefits payable by a union due to a labor dispute are exempt without making a claim. Cal. Civ. Proc. Code § 704.120(b).

5. Benefits from disability or health insurance policies are exempt. Cal. Civ. Proc. Code § 704.130(a).

6. There is an absolute exemption for a cause of action for personal injury. Award of damages or settlement from a personal injury claim is exempt to the extent necessary for the support of you and dependents. Cal. Civ. Proc. Code § 704.140(a).

7. There is an absolute exemption for a cause of action for wrongful death. An award of damages or settlement rising out of a wrongful death action is exempt to the extent reasonably necessary for support of you and dependents. Cal. Civ. Proc. Code § 704.150(a) and (b). Wrongful death claim must be for your spouse or person for whom the worker's compensation is exempt. Cal. Civ. Proc. Code § 704.160(a).

8. Payment of Social Securities or social services aid is exempt. Cal. Civ. Proc. Code § 704.170.

9. Relocation benefits for displacement from a dwelling are exempt. Cal. Civ. Proc. Code § 704.180.

10. Financial aid for expenses while attending an institution of higher education is exempt. Cal. Civ. Proc. Code § 704.190.

11. There is an absolute exemption for unmatured life insurance policies. The aggregate loan value of such a policy is exempt in the amount of $11,475. The exemption of spouses may be combined regardless of the ownership of the policies. Benefits from matured life insurance policies are exempt to an extent reasonably necessary for the support of you and dependents. Cal. Civ. Proc. Code § 704.100.

12. Funds held in a trust account by the state, county, or city for the benefit of a debtor confined in prison are exempt in an amount not to exceed $1,425. Cal. Civ. Proc. Code § 704.090.

13. Any benefits payable under the public employees retirement system, county employees retirement fund, county peace officers retirement fund, or county fire service retirement fund are exempt. CGC §§ 31452, 31913, and 32210.

ALTERNATIVE II:

The exemptions available to you under the alternative set of California state law exemptions are similar to the exemptions available under federal law and are generally as follows:

Homestead Exemption.

You can take the following exemption for your homestead (your home and adjacent land):

Your aggregate interest, not to exceed seventeen thousand

four hundred twenty-five dollars ($17,425) in value, in real property or personal property that you or a dependent use as a residence, in a cooperative that owns property that you or a dependent use as a residence, or in a burial plot for you or a dependent. Cal. Civ. Proc. Code § 704.140(b)(1).

Personal Property.

You can exempt the following personal property:

1. Motor vehicle up to $3,525. Cal. Civ. Proc. Code § 703.140(b)(2).

2. Clothing, household goods, appliances, furnishings, animals, books, musical instruments and crops up to $550 per item. Cal. Civ. Proc. Code § 703.140(b)(3).

3. Jewelry up to $1,425. Cal. Civ. Proc. Code § 703.140(b)(4).

4. $15,000 of any property, less any claim for homestead or burial plot. Cal. Civ. Proc. Code § 703.140(b)(5).

5. Tools, books and implements of trade up to $2,200.. Cal. Civ. Proc. Code § 703.140(b)(6).

Benefits and Insurance.

You can exempt the following benefits and insurance:

1. Any unmatured life insurance contract owned by the debtor, other than a credit life insurance contract. Cal. Civ. Proc. Code § 703.140(b)(7).

2. Your aggregate interest, not to exceed $11,800, in any accrued dividend or interest under, or loan value of, any unmatured life insurance contract. Cal. Civ. Proc. Code § 703.140(b)(7).

3. Your right to receive any of the following:

(A) A social security benefit, unemployment compensation, or a local public assistance benefit.

(B) A veterans' benefit.

(C) A disability, illness, or unemployment benefit.

(D) Alimony, support, or separate maintenance, to the extent reasonably necessary for support.

(E) A payment under a stock bonus, pension, profit-sharing, annuity, or similar plan or contract on account of illness, disability, death, age, or length of service, to the extent reasonably necessary for support unless all of the following apply:

(i) That plan or contract was established by or under the auspices of an insider that employed you at the time your rights under the plan or contract arose.

(ii) The payment is on account of age or length of service.

(iii) That plan or contract does not qualify under Section 401(a), 403(a), 403(b), 408, or 408A of the Internal Revenue Code of 1986.

4. Your right to receive, or property that is traceable to, any of the following:

(A) An award under a crime victim's reparation law.

(B) A payment on account of the wrongful death of an individual reasonably necessary for support. Cal. Civ. Proc. Code § 703.140(b)(11).

(C) A payment under a life insurance contract that insured the life of an individual reasonably necessary for support. § 703.140(b) (11).

(D) A payment, not to exceed $22,075, on account of personal bodily injury, not including pain and suffering or compensation for actual pecuniary loss, of you or a dependent. Cal. Civ. Proc. Code. § 703.140(b) (11).

E) A payment in compensation of loss of future earnings of you or a dependent, to

the extent reasonably necessary for the support you or a dependent. § 703.140(b) (11).

5. Professionally prescribed health aids for you or a dependent. Cal. Civ. Proc. Code § 703.140(b)(9).

Pensions

1. ERISA-qualified benefits needed for support. Cal. Civ. Proc. Code § 703.140(b)(10).

2. Tax exempt retirement accounts (including 401(k)s, 403(b)s, profit-sharing and money purchase plans, SEP and SIMPLE IRAs, and defined benefit plans). 11 U.S.C. § 522 -

3. IRAs and Roth IRAs to $1,171,150. 11 U.S.C. § 522(b)(3)(C)(n) -

Wildcard

$1,100 of any property. The unused portion of the burial or household exemption for any property. Cal. Civ. Proc. Code § 703.140(b)(5).

Note: Some supplemental federal exemptions may be available to you when choosing the state law exemptions.

HOMESTEADS: The exemption for a homestead is limited to $146,450 if the property was acquired within the previous 1215 day (3.3 years). This cap is not applicable to any interest transferred from your previous principal residence (which was acquired prior to the beginning of such 1215-day period.

The value of the state homestead exemption is reduced by any addition to the value brought if you disposed any nonexempt property (made with the intent to hinder, delay, or defraud creditors) during the 10 years prior to the bankruptcy filing.

An absolute $146,450 homestead cap applies if either:

The court determines that you have been convicted of a felony demonstrating that the filing of the case was an abuse of the provision of the Bankruptcy Code; or

You owe a debt arising from a violation of federal or state securities laws, fiduciary fraud, racketeering, or crimes or intentional torts that caused serious bodily injury or death in the preceding 5 years.

NOTE: This limitation is inapplicable if the homestead property is reasonably necessary for your support and any dependent.

****Make sure you comply with the filing requirements (if necessary) to declare a homestead in California BEFORE you file your bankruptcy case.****

Chapter 10

WHAT ARE THE DIFFERENT TYPES OF DEBTS?

In bankruptcy, debts are divided into four categories: secured, unsecured, priority and administrative debts. The different types of debts receive different treatment in bankruptcy cases. Unsecured debts can be generally discharged in your bankruptcy case (except those "non-dischargeable" debts discussed in Chapter 11 of this Guide) while secured debts, priority debts, and administrative debts generally require heightened treatment which may include payment in full.

Secured Debt: A secured debt is a debt collateralized by the debtor's property, such as a car. A debtor is the one who owes the money to another person, know as a creditor. A creditor whose debt is secured has a right to take collateral to satisfy the debt. For example, people who buy cars on credit are debtors. They give the lender, the creditor, a "security interest" (or lien) in the car. The car is the collateral for the loan and the debt is deemed "secured" by the car. The lender can take (repossess) the car if the borrower fails to make payments on the loan.

Unsecured Debt: A debt for which the creditor has no security interest (lien) with which to satisfy the debt is known as unsecured. The debt is said to be a general unsecured debt if the claim is also not entitled to any priority of payment under the Bankruptcy Code. For example, the amount owed on a credit card is an unsecured debt.

Priority Debt: A priority debt is a debt entitled to priority in payment, ahead of most other debts, in a bankruptcy case.

Examples of priority debts are some taxes, wage claims of employees, and alimony, maintenance or support of a spouse, former spouse, or child.

Administrative Debt: This type of debt arises after the bankruptcy case is filed. An administrative debt is a priority debt created when someone provides goods or services to your bankruptcy estate. Examples of an administrative debt are the fees generated by the trustee in representing the bankruptcy estate.

Chapter 11

WHAT HAPPENS TO NON-DISCHARGEABLE DEBTS?

Non-dischargeable debts will not be affected by a bankruptcy filing, and you will still have to pay them in full.

The following is a list of the most common non-dischargeable debts.

Domestic Support Obligations (alimony, maintenance and child support);

Certain types of taxes owed within 3 years of your bankruptcy filing;

Debts incurred by the use of false financial statements or other false pretenses;

Court fines and penalties, including criminal fines and restitution to court or a victim imposed in criminal type proceeding;

Cash advances on credit cards in last 60 days; credit card purchases more than $1,075 for luxury goods or services in last 60 days;

Debts arising from a judgment incurred from a DWI/DUI conviction;

Damages arising from willful or malicious injury to property or persons;

Federally insured student loans, unless you can show undue hardship;

Debts arising from fraud or embezzlement or from the misuse of funds when you were acting as a fiduciary or caretaker of other people's funds;

Credit card charges for payment of taxes to the IRS;

Debts from marital settlement agreement or divorce decree;

Debts owed to certain tax-advantaged retirement plans;

Debts for certain condominium or cooperative housing fees;

Debts you couldn't discharge in a previous bankruptcy that was dismissed due to fraud or malfeasance.

You must pay particular attention to your non-dischargeable debts and how they are affecting you financially.

If your non-dischargeable debts are the root of your financial problems, filing a bankruptcy case may not be a good alternative for you.

Still, even when you have non-dischargeable debts, you should evaluate your entire financial picture, and use this guide to weigh all the pros and cons of a bankruptcy filing.

If you do not have any non-dischargeable debts, all of your debts are capable of being discharged in your bankruptcy case, but exceptions may still exist, such as secured loans and priority debts. Double-check the list of the most common non-dischargeable debts to ensure you have no non-dischargeable debts.

Chapter 12

WHAT HAPPENS TO YOUR HOME?

If you own a home and that you want to keep it, bankruptcy should be a last resort.

If your only financial problem is your mortgage, you should likely avoid filing a bankruptcy case and seek to modify your mortgage to make it more affordable through your lender and some of the government programs. You can enter into a mortgage modification program, including HAMP (Home Affordable Modification Program) and others established by the Obama administration, then you may be able to reduce the principal, the interest rate or both, bringing your monthly mortgage payment down to a more affordable level. This is the best result if you are an "underwater" homeowner, that is, you owe more on your house than its fair market value.

Other options include working out a short sale with your lender or "walking away" from your house and leaving it in your lender's hands. Remember, if you walk away, you may be personally liable for the portion of your loan that exceeds the price your lender gets from the sale of your home. Alaska, Arizona, California, Connecticut, Florida, Idaho, Minnesota, North Carolina, North Dakota, Texas, Utah and Washington are generally non-recourse states where a lender cannot sue you for additional funds over the value of the sale price of the home.

Considering Bankruptcy When you Own a Home

If financial problems with your home are coupled with overall financial problems and mortgage modification is not working or your lender will not agree to work with you,

you could consider either a Chapter 7 or a Chapter 13 bankruptcy case.

You will only be able to keep your home in a Chapter 7 bankruptcy case if you are current on your mortgage, continue to make payments as contracted and enter into a workout or reaffirmation agreement with your lender. If you can continue to make payments in a Chapter 7 bankruptcy case, you can reduce any second mortgages or home equity lines that are not secured (i.e., all the equity of the house is eaten up by the first mortgage) into general unsecured claim, for which personal liability can be discharged in the Chapter 7 bankruptcy case with other unsecured debts for a very small percentage of the debt or for nothing at all. However, the lien on the house remains, so that when the house is sold, the second mortgagee or home equity line lender could look for their payoff to discharge its mortgage.

In a Chapter 13 bankruptcy case, you can retain your home by paying the mortgage by its terms after filing your bankruptcy case. The advantage on a Chapter 13 bankruptcy case is that you have the opportunity to pay off any defaults on your mortgage over three to five years through your Chapter 13 bankruptcy plan. You also have the ability to "strip-off" any second mortgages and home equity lines that are completely unsecured, provided you do not default during the Chapter 13 plan.

While bankruptcy generally relieves some pressure and will give you time to make some decisions, bankruptcy may not be the best option for a homeowner and should only be considered as a last option.

At a minimum, bankruptcy will provide you some breathing room and temporarily stall a foreclosure sale.

In a Chapter 7 bankruptcy case, the automatic stay temporarily prevents a foreclosure process from continuing.

Your mortgage lender can continue the foreclosure process with the permission of the court, but that usually takes at least 60 days. You can use this time to work out a loan modification.

In a Chapter 13 bankruptcy case, the automatic stay likewise temporarily prevents your lender from continuing a foreclosure process, so that you can regroup and work out a way to keep your home. In addition, you can cure a default or pay off the mortgage in installments payments over time through a chapter 13 plan.

In all bankruptcy cases, you may be able to respond to your mortgage lender's claims about how much you owe.

Chapter 13

WHAT HAPPENS TO YOUR CAR, TRUCK, RV OR BOAT?

Because of the automatic stay, filing a bankruptcy case stops your lender from seizing your vehicle. Bankruptcy halts all attempts to take any of your property, even property on which your lenders have liens. Moreover, if your car has been repossessed but not sold, bankruptcy may help you get your car back. Bankruptcy also provides ways to keep your car for the long term.

In a Chapter 7 Bankruptcy Case

At the beginning of your Chapter 7 bankruptcy case, you must file a document called a Statement of Intention. In this Statement, you must tell the court what you plan to do with any secured collateral such as your car.

In a Chapter 7 bankruptcy case, you can "redeem" your vehicle, "reaffirm" your debt or surrender the vehicle. A fourth option, doing nothing and continuing to pay the loan, may also exist, but it's questionable and depends on obtaining the consent of the lender. If you do not act in accordance with the Statement, the lender that holds the security interest on that collateral will not be barred by the automatic stay of picking up that collateral 30 days after the Section 341 creditors meeting.

Moreover, bankruptcy also provides you the ability to challenge your auto debt or a repossession to ensure that they were lawful in form and execution.

Redemption

To redeem your car in bankruptcy, you pay your lender only what the car is worth, not what you owe on your loan.

Redemption in bankruptcy can save you considerable funds from redemption outside of bankruptcy. Outside of bankruptcy, to redeem you have to pay your entire loan, including all costs and fees in order to redeem. In bankruptcy, you redeem at the replacement value without deducting for the costs of sale. If your car is worth $10,000, but you still owe $15,000 on your loan, you only have to pay $10,000 to redeem the car in bankruptcy.

Example Vehicle Redemption

If you owned a 2007 F150, the vehicle redemption might be as follows:

> *Kelly Blue Book Value: $12,000*
> *Outstanding Balance on Loan: $17,000*
> *You Pay to Redeem Outside of Bankruptcy: $17,000*
> *You Pay in Full to Redeem During Bankruptcy: $12,000*

You must pay the entire redemption amount in cash. Some creditors let you redeem in installment payments, but the bankruptcy court cannot require a lender to accept installment payments. Also, some lenders may offer you a loan for the present value of your car, so you can redeem in your bankruptcy case. These are called "redemption" loans. You may find this new loan with a much lower principal very appealing, especially if you can value your car at a depressed level and are able to refinance again in the future. However, beware of interest rates and fees included in the redemption loan.

Reaffirmation

When you enter into a reaffirmation agreement, you agree to repay a debt that would otherwise be discharged in your bankruptcy case. Your personal liability on your auto loan would normally be discharged in bankruptcy, but your lender would continue to have the right to repossess. You would reaffirm an auto loan in order to keep a car in which a lender has a security interest.

You must meet certain requirements to enter into a reaffirmation agreement. First, your reaffirmation must be effective under non-bankruptcy law and the creditor must make numerous disclosures of the costs of reaffirmation. Second, you must enter into the reaffirmation agreement before you receive a discharge in your bankruptcy case. In addition, the bankruptcy court will often approve your reaffirmation only if you appear before the bankruptcy court for a hearing. At this time, you will be told that no discharge debt, such as your auto loan, must be reaffirmed. In addition, the bankruptcy judge will tell you the consequences of entering into a reaffirmation agreement, including repossession and a deficiency judgment if you default.

Because bankruptcy law seeks to protect lenders from pressuring debtors into a reaffirmation of an auto loan, reaffirmation requirements include:

An agreement be executed before discharge;
The debtor's right to rescind for 60 days;
Lenders provide specific disclosures;
An agreement be filed with the bankruptcy court;
That the debtor appear at a hearing in front of a
bankruptcy judge if not represented by a lawyer;
A lawyer's signature if represented by a lawyer.

Make sure that you can make the monthly payments, because if you breach an approved reaffirmation agreement, you will still owe the entire debt, including any deficiency after the sale of the vehicle, notwithstanding the bankruptcy discharge.

If you have an attorney, your attorney must file an affidavit stating that your reaffirmation is voluntary and does not impose an undue hardship on you. You must disclose your income and expenses reflecting your ability to pay the reaffirmed debt, unless the lender is a credit union. If you are without an attorney, the bankruptcy court must evaluate whether the agreement will impose undue hardship on you and that the agreement is in your best interests, and the court will not approve the agreement if it is not in your interest.

Bankruptcy courts are generally reluctant to allow you to enter into a reaffirmation agreement when you want to reaffirm to keep driving a luxury car. Also, they hesitate to allow you to enter into reaffirmation agreement if you seek to protect the guarantee of a friend or relative. Even if you meet all the requirements of a reaffirmation agreement, you get a 60-day cooling off period in which you are free to rescind the reaffirmation.

Consider all alternatives before reaffirming a debt such as an auto loan, and seriously consider selling your car and replacing it with a less expensive used car before you enter into a reaffirmation agreement.

Treatment of Vehicle Loans in Chapter 13

In a Chapter 13 case, your best bet is to pay off your car in monthly payments in three to five years through your Chapter 13 plan. You may be able to reduce your interest rate in the plan and potentially reduce what you owe on the current value of the car if your loan is not a purchase money security interest on a car purchased within 910 days before the bankruptcy.

For purchase money security interests on vehicle purchases less than 910 days before bankruptcy, the vehicle loan must be paid in full either over the life of the plan, or according to the terms of the loan agreement. You should determine which option presents the most affordable method to pay your vehicle debts and draft the Chapter 13 plan accordingly.

Vehicle Leases in Bankruptcy

Before you take any actions in bankruptcy regarding your vehicle lease, you must make sure that you have a true lease rather then a "rent to own" transaction.

You likely entered into a true lease if your financing entity actually owns the vehicle, and at the end of the term, you have nothing. You have to return the vehicle and you cannot sell the vehicle. Under a true lease agreement, the terms of the lease contract govern the rights and obligations between you and the lender. Typically your vehicle lessor has the right to repossess the car for any default, such as nonpayment of an installment or lack of insurance, the same manner as a secured party would.

In a bankruptcy case, you can assume the vehicle lease, meaning you can agree to continue with the lease and cure defaults, or reject the lease, meaning that you can surrender the vehicle and have no further obligation to pay lease installments. If you do not expressly reject or assume your vehicle lease within 60 days of filing in a Chapter 7 bankruptcy case, the lease is rejected by operation of law. Your vehicle lessor is entitled to repossess the vehicle without seeking relief from the automatic stay. In bankruptcy cases in all chapters, you must indicate in your initial bankruptcy documents your intent to assume your vehicle lease.

Chapter 14

SAMPLE CHAPTER 13 BANKRUPTCY PLAN

Following is a modified sample template of a Chapter 13 plan from the United States Bankruptcy Court for the District of Massachusetts for your reference. I believe the Massachusetts form presents a good overview of what to expect when drafting your Chapter 13 plan.

Most bankruptcy courts throughout the country have preferred forms which you can obtain from the bankruptcy court or online at the bankruptcy court's website. Call or go online to see if the bankruptcy court where you must file your case has a local form, and use that form if you do decide to file a Chapter 13 bankruptcy case.

SAMPLE CHAPTER 13 PLAN:

DEBTOR(S):

(H)_____ SS#: _____

(W)_____ SS#: _____

I. PLAN PAYMENT AND TERM:

Debtor(s) shall pay monthly to the Trustee the sum of $_____ for the term of:

☐ ___ 36 Months. 11 U.S.C. 1325(b)(4)(A)(i);

☐ ___ 60 Months. 11 U.S.C. 1325(b)(4)(A)(ii);

☐ ___ 60 Months. 11 U.S.C. 1322(d)(2). The Debtor avers the following cause:

_____
_____; or

☐ _____ Months. The Debtor states as reasons
therefore:

_____
_____

II. SECURED CLAIMS:

A. Claims to be paid through the plan (including arrears):

List each *Creditor* with a Secured Claim, a *Description of Claim* (pre-petition arrears, purchase money, etc.), and the *Amount of Claim.*

Total the secured claims to be paid through the Plan:
$_____.

B. Claims to be paid directly by debtor to creditors (Not through Plan):

List each *Creditor* with a secured claim not being paid through the Plan and a *Description of each Claim.*

C. Modification of Secured Claims:

List each *Creditor* with a modified secured claim, the *Details of Modification*, and the *Amount of each Claim to Be Paid Through Plan.*

D. Leases:

i. The Debtor(s) intend(s) to reject the residential/personal property lease claims of

_____; or

ii. The Debtor(s) intend(s) to assume the residential/personal property lease claims of

_____.

iii. The arrears under the lease to be paid under the plan are

_____.

III. PRIORITY CLAIMS:

A. Domestic Support Obligations:

List each *Creditor* to whom you owe a domestic support obligation, a *Description of each Claim*, and the *Amount of Claim.*

B. Other Priority Claims:

List each *Creditor* with another priority claim, a *Description of the Claim*, and the *Amount of Claim.*

Total of Priority Claims to Be Paid Through the Plan: $_____.

IV. ADMINISTRATIVE CLAIMS:

A. *Attorneys Fees* (to be paid through the plan):$_____.

B. *Miscellaneous Fees:*

List each *Creditor* and a *Description of each Claim*, and the *Amount of Claim.*

C. The *Chapter 13 Trustee's fee* is determined by Order of the United States Attorney General. The calculation of the Plan Payment set forth utilizes a 10% Trustee's commission.

V. UNSECURED CLAIMS:

The general unsecured creditors shall receive a dividend of _____% of their claims.

A. *General unsecured claims* $_____

B. *Undersecured claims arising after lien avoidance/cramdown:*

List each *Creditor* with an undersecured claim, a *Description of each Claim*, and the *Amount of Claim*.

C. *Non-Dischargeable Unsecured Claims:*

List each *Creditor* with a non-dischargeable unsecured claim, a *Description of each Claim*, and the *Amount of Claim.*

Total of Unsecured Claims (A + B + C):
$_____

D. *Multiply total by percentage set forth above*:
$_____

(Example: Total of $38,500.00 x .22 dividend = $8,470.00)

E. Separately classified unsecured claims (co-borrower, etc.):

List each *Creditor* with a separately classified unsecured claim, a *Description of each Claim*, and the *Amount of Claim.*

Total amount of separately classified claims payable at _____%: $_____.

VI. OTHER PROVISIONS:

A. Liquidation of assets to be used to fund plan:

_____
_____.

B. Miscellaneous Provisions:

_____
_____.

VII. CALCULATION OF PLAN PAYMENT:

a) Secured claims (Section I-A Total): $_____

b) Priority claims (Section II-A & B Total): $_____

c) Administrative claims (Section III-A&B Total): +$_____

d) Regular unsecured claims (Section IV-D Total): +$_____

e) Separately classified unsecured claims: $_____

f) Total of a + b + c + d + e above: = $_____

g) Divide (f) by .90 for total including Trustee's fee:

Cost of Plan = $_____

(This represents the total amount to be paid into the Chapter 13 Plan.)

h) Divide (g), Cost of Plan, by Term of Plan, __months.

i) Round up to nearest dollar for Monthly Plan Payment: $____ (Enter this amount on page 1).

Pursuant to 11 U.S.C. sec. 1326(a)(1) unless the Court orders otherwise, debtor shall commence making the payments proposed by a plan within thirty (30) days after the petition is filed.

Pursuant to 11 U.S.C. sec. 1326(a)(1)(C), the debtor shall make pre-confirmation adequate protection payments directly to the secured creditor.

VIII. LIQUIDATION ANALYSIS

A. Real Estate:

List the *Address*, the *Fair Market Value*, and the *Total Amount of Recorded Liens (Schedule D)* for each real property

Total the Net Equity for Real Property: $_____.

Less Total Exemptions (Schedule C):$ _____.

Amount Available in Chapter 7: $_____.

B. Automobile (Describe year, make, model):

List the *Value*, the *Lien Amount* and the *Exemption Amount* for each automobile.

Total the Net Equity for Automobiles: $_____.

Less Total Exemptions (Schedule C): $ _____.

Amount Available in a Chapter 7: $_____.

C. All other Assets: (All remaining items on schedule B): (Itemize as necessary)

_____
_____
_____.

Total the Net Equity for All other Assets:
$_____.

Less Total Exemptions (Schedule C):$ _____.

Amount Available in a Chapter 7: $_____.

D. Summary of foregoing Liquidation Analysis (total amount available under Chapter 7):

_____

Net Equity (A and B) plus Other Assets (C) less all claimed exemptions: $_____.

E. Additional Comments regarding Liquidation Analysis:

_____

_____.

IX. SIGNATURES.

Pursuant to the Chapter 13 rules, the debtor or his or her attorney is required to serve a copy of the Plan upon the Chapter 13 Trustee, all creditors and interested parties, and to file a Certificate of Service accordingly.

/s/Debtor's Attorney, Date.
Attorney's Address.
Tel. #.
Email Address.

I/WE DECLARE UNDER THE PENALTIES OF PERJURY THAT THE FOREGOING REPRESENTATIONS OF FACT ARE TRUE AND CORRECT TO THE BEST OF OUR KNOWLEDGE AND BELIEF.

/s/ Debtor, Date.

Chapter 15

ALTERNATIVES TO A BANKRUPTCY CASE

Before you file for bankruptcy, make sure you consider all of the options available to you and make an informed choice. I highly recommend that you consult the book, _The Road Out of Debt: Bankruptcy and Other Solutions to Your Financial Problems_ to ensure you have considered all options and to learn how you may be able to deal with your debts without filing for bankruptcy. The book also provides great hypothetical stories of real bankruptcy cases that prepare you for a worst case scenario of what can happen in a bankruptcy case. After reading the worst case scenario, your bankruptcy case will feel like a breeze (most likely it will be anyway, if you follow the instructions in this guide and advice in the book). Here are some alternatives to consider:

Do Nothing

Doing nothing seems unusual, but it is often the least expensive and easiest option for someone in financial trouble. If you have no assets that creditors can get, you are "judgment proof." If you are judgment proof, you should consider not filing bankruptcy at all, but instead write letters to your creditors stating that you are judgment proof. Although only a bankruptcy will stop collection efforts as a matter of law, many creditors can be persuaded with a letter that they should abandon the effort to collect assets from a judgment proof individual. The letter should say that your creditor should stop contacting you, that you may file for bankruptcy, in which event your case will be closed as a "no asset" case, and that it is futile for the creditor to continue its collection efforts. Failure of a creditor to cease collection efforts after the letter may subject the creditor to liability for violating Fair Debt Collection Practices Act (FDCPA).

Credit Counseling

Many good credit counselors will do their best to help you avoid filing for bankruptcy. However, some credit counselors are bad and will just collect money for you without providing any valuable services. Be careful when hiring a credit counselor. Look for accredited non-profits and HUD- approved housing counselors.

Workouts

Direct workouts, *i.e.* negotiations directly with creditors, may be a way to resolve your financial problems. There are numerous types of workouts that often depend on creditor's policies. You may be able to work out a repayment plan for some or all of the debt over time with a reduced interest rate that could include forgiveness of some or all of your debt.

Loan Modifications

As a homeowner, you can try various measures to avoid foreclosure outside of bankruptcy; however, all require some type of concession by the home mortgage company. Loan modifications are specific to each homeowner and lender and involve a negotiation of workout terms. The government has been pressuring mortgage lenders to enter into modifications but they are still hard to obtain. Hopefully, this situation will change soon. Nevertheless, it is a good avenue to pursue.

Refinancing

Refinancing debts through the equity in your home, such as through a second mortgage, reverse mortgage or home equity line, are also alternatives to bankruptcy. If you have equity and can get decent rates, you should consider these options but beware the increased risk that you are losing equity and increasing the risk of losing your home.

Foreclosure Rescue

Watch Out for Scams! Never pursue a foreclosure rescue transaction in order to avoid bankruptcy. Never transfer your house to another individual or company who promises to refinance it and pay your mortgage. These deals are always scams. Transferring the title to your home or property is permanent and fraught with danger. I've seen too many rescues go extremely bad. Stay far away.

Chapter 16

10 MYTHS ABOUT FILING FOR BANKRUPTCY

1.) I won't owe any more debts. Not all debts are discharged, which means they stay with you regardless of filing for bankruptcy. Some of these debts include alimony, child support and most taxes.

2.) Only the poor file for bankruptcy. Everyone, no matter how rich, may file a bankruptcy case. Look at the most successful real estate broker in Orange County. The poor usually don't (and probably shouldn't) file for bankruptcy, because they are likely judgment proof, so any creditor claims against them would be impossible to collect.

3.) I'll lose everything. You have exempt assets that will definitely stay yours. You can also keep other assets by continuing to pay or working out a plan.

4.) My credit score will never recover. Your credit score will drop, but you can rebuild it with consistent payments on new loans or secured credit cards.

5.) Bankruptcy's too hard under the new laws. Bankruptcy has not changed drastically. The filing documents are a bit bothersome and you have two credit counseling financial management classes to take.

6.) There's no reason to file in a recovering economy. Maybe not, but filing for bankruptcy should depend on your own personal finances, not the economy.

7.) **My life as I know it will end if I file.** This too shall pass. Plus, the only people who will likely find out are those you tell.

8.) **A debt settlement firm will bail me out.** No way. Too many so-called debt settlement firms will take your money and do little or nothing for your debts.

9.) **I can hide property in my bankruptcy.** Just ask former Major League Baseball All Star Lenny Dykstra, who is indicted for bankruptcy fraud, people do find out about property you omit from your bankruptcy forms and documents. Be honest or don't file.

10.) **Filing for bankruptcy must be cheap, or even, free.** Unfortunately, it's not. As strange as it seems, bankruptcy costs money and you should probably save up for a lawyer. If you really need it, you may be able to get help from bankruptcy court.

Chapter 17

RESOURCES

This guide gives you the essentials of what you need for a bankruptcy filing. While it gets you on your way and puts you ahead of most debtors, this guide does not cover all contingencies in a bankruptcy case and you may want more information.

In particular, I recommend:

The Road Out of Debt: Bankruptcy and Other Solutions to Your Financial Problems by Joan N. Feeney and me (Wiley & Sons, Inc. 2010); This book will answer your questions about all different types of debt relief and help you decide whether you need to file bankruptcy or if better solutions are available. An exceptional resource that offers real solutions that you won't find in most books.

"The last thing your creditors want you to do is buy [*The Road out of Debt*]. Why? Because it gives you essential, easy-to-understand and practical tools for getting out of debt." Gary B. Smith, Fox Business News.

For Lawyers and Other Professionals:

I strongly recommend the Bankruptcy Law Manual by the Hon. Nancy C. Dreher and Hon. Joan N. Feeney (West 2011). This authoritative desk reference manual designed for business or consumer bankruptcy specialists as well as general practitioners contains numerous practice pointers and authoritative commentary while covering issues common to all types of bankruptcy cases.

Additionally, here are other great sources:

Bankruptcy and Debt Basics

American Association of Retired Persons (AARP): www.aarp.org

American Bankruptcy Institute: www.abiworld.org.

The Center for Responsible Lending: www.responsiblelending.org.

Elizabeth Warren's works (Harvard Law professor and bankruptcy expert): www.law.harvard.edu/faculty/directory/facdir.php?id=82)

Jump$tart Coalition for Personal Financial Literacy: www.jumpstartcoalition.org

LegalConsumer.com- a great website for more of the same information provided in this Guide.

Practical Money Skills: www.practicalmoneyskills.com

U.S. Bankruptcy Courts: www.uscourts.gov/bankruptcycourts/bankruptcybasics.html

Consumer Credit Debt

National Foundation for Consumer Credit (NFCC): (800) 388-2227 or www.nfcc.org. See www.nfcc.org/FirstStep/firststep_01.cfm for a list of NFCC-approved counselors.

Association of Independent Consumer Credit Counseling Agencies (AICCCA): (866) 703-8787 or www.aiccca.org. See www.aiccca.org/find.cfm for a list of AICCCA-approved counselors.

Better Business Bureau (BBB): (703) 276.0100 or www.bbb.org. See www.bbb.org/us/ to ensure that other consumers have not had difficulties with the credit counselor you are considering hiring.

Stop receiving pre-screened credit card offers by notifying each of the three major credit bureaus, Equifax, Experian, and Trans Union, through their websites:

Equifax: www.equifax.com

Experian: www.experian.com

TransUnion: www.transunion.com

Legal Help

Contact the clerk of the bankruptcy court, the U.S. Trustee's Office or the office of the bankruptcy administrator in your area and ask for names of competent consumer bankruptcy lawyers.

American Bar Association: www.abalawinfo.org /find1.html and www.abanet.org/legalservices/findlegalhelp/home.cfm (American Bar Association list of resources including foreclosure resources and information)

American Bankruptcy Institute: www.abiworld.org

Martindale Hubbell lawyer rating service: www.martindale.com

National Association of Consumer Bankruptcy Attorneys: www.nacba.org

National Consumer Law Center: www.consumerlaw.org or www.nclc.org.

Thomson West Publications attorney locator service: www.findlaw.com and bankruptcy.findlaw.com

USCourts.gov's publication Filing for Bankruptcy without an Attorney: This resource provides more detailed information about the procedures for filing for bankruptcy for the individual who chooses to represent him or herself.

Mortgage Debt

The following resources are useful in dealing with mortgage debt, foreclosure, or mortgage scams.

Comptroller of the Currency U.S. Department of the Treasury: www.helpwithmybank.gov www.occ.treas.gov.

Federal Deposit Insurance Corporation (FDIC): www.fdic.gov;

Federal Housing Administration (FHA): 1 (800) CALL-FHA or www.fha.com

Federal Trade Commission (FTC): www.ftc.gov/bcp/edu/pubs/consumer/homes/rea04.shtm

Federal Reserve Board: www.federalreserve.gov/pubs/foreclosurescamtips/default.htm

Homeowner Crisis Resource Center: www.housinghelpnow.org

Homeownership Preservation Foundation (HPF) and HOPE NOW hotline: (888) 995-HOPE or www.hopenow.com

Making Home Affordable: www.makinghomeaffordable.gov

NeighborWorks America: www.nw.org/network/home.asp

The Office of the Comptroller of the Currency (OCC): www.helpwithmybank.gov and www.occ.gov/customer.htm.

U.S. Department of Housing and Urban Development (HUD): (800) 569-4287 or www.hud.gov. See www.hud.gov/offices/hsg/sfh/hcc/hccprof14.cfm for a list of HUD-approved counselors.

THANK YOU!

Thank you for buying this guide and considering this advice on bankruptcy. I sincerely hope you succeed in solving your financial issues. I know how tough and debilitating dealing with debts can be, which is why I have made it my mission to help as many people as I can get on their own personal road out of debt.

I would be thrilled to hear about your successes or help you overcome any roadblocks and hurdles you may face. Please visit www.roadoutofdebt.com or www.theodoreconnolly.com and click on the "Contact" button. We can start a great relationship to help in our fights against debt. Plus, you can join the website community to hook up with others who have started their own battles out of debt. You can read my blog and visit www.filingmadesimple.com. The blog and the websites provide information, insight and inspiration to help you battle your way out of debt.

Best wishes, always.

Ted

While this guide provides you with the basics of what you need to know, bankruptcy law and your situation change constantly. This personalized guide is for informational purposes only and cannot be relied upon for anything other than what you can generally expect to happen to you and your assets based on other debtors in similar situations to yours.

This guide is intended as a general discussion of legal issues regarding your assets and debt and not as a statement of fact, legal advice or a legal opinion. Personal opinions may also be expressed. No attorney-client relationship is created by this guide. Do not act or rely upon law-related information in this guide without seeking the advice of an attorney licensed to practice in debt and bankruptcy areas, preferably with experience with bankruptcy cases.

www.ingramcontent.com/pod-product-compliance
Lightning Source LLC
Chambersburg PA
CBHW051344170526
45166CB00002B/956